W9-BUD-584

IMAGES
of America

CHARLOTTE
ITS HISTORIC
NEIGHBORHOODS

IMAGES
of America

CHARLOTTE
ITS HISTORIC
NEIGHBORHOODS

John R. Rogers and Amy T. Rogers

NEW HANOVER COUNTY
PUBLIC LIBRARY
201 CHESTNUT STREET
WILMINGTON, N. C. 28401

ARCADIA

First published 1996
Copyright © John R. Rogers and Amy T. Rogers, 1996

ISBN 0-7524-0515-2

Published by Arcadia Publishing,
an imprint of Tempus Publishing, Inc.
2 Cumberland Street, Charleston SC 29401.
Printed in Great Britain

Library of Congress Cataloging-in-Publication Data applied for

This book is dedicated to our parents
John and Mary Ann Rogers
and to the memory of Marshall and Elaine Rogers.
No connection to history is stronger than that through our families.

Contents

Charlotte's trolley last ran on March 14, 1938. During the 1930s, the Duke Power Company had successfully petitioned the State Utilities Commission and the Charlotte City Council to allow the replacement of the city's street railroads with a bus system that would be phased in throughout town. This memorable image shows the crowd of citizens and dignitaries that turned out to meet the last trolley at the Square. For more than four decades, the trolley was a part of daily life in Charlotte. The farewell event marked the end of an era, and a shift in the character of the city. (Robinson-Spangler Carolina Room, Public Library of Charlotte and Mecklenburg County)

Cover photograph courtesy of the Robinson-Spangler Carolina Room, Public Library of Charlotte and Mecklenburg County.

Introduction

Charlotte, North Carolina, in many ways embodies the character and history of the South. It is a city that has humble, almost accidental beginnings, yet it has grown to be a major business and financial center. It has often wrestled with its own legacy, and at many points in its past it has sought to rewrite its future. Today, Charlotte stands as one of the fastest growing cities in the Southeast.

Charlotte's origins lie in its location at a crossroads of two routes important in the early history of the region. Here, a Native American trading path passed through the domain of the Catawbas, between Charleston on the South Carolina coast and the Cherokee Nation to the west. It was a major trade route between the new Carolina colony, with its European connections, and the Native American peoples. At what would become Charlotte, the path was crossed by the Great Wagon Road, a major migration route south from the new European colonies to the north. These two roads became Trade and Tryon Streets and defined what is still known today as "the Square."

The two streets divided the village into four wards, and these became Charlotte's first neighborhoods. The wards surrounded the Mecklenburg County Courthouse, located at the Square, and a healthy business community grew near the crossroads. The four wards, each with its own character and yet also dependent on the others, remained the only neighborhoods in Charlotte for generations, each residence within a short walk of all others, and all focused on the town center.

For more than a century since its incorporation in 1768, Charlotte grew slowly, with an economy fueled by the surrounding agrarian culture and by the small business activity usually found around county seats. The discovery of gold in the region led to the establishment of a branch of the United States Mint in Charlotte in 1837, and the arrival of the railroad soon after ensured Charlotte's future as a transportation center. This heritage continues today as the city is located at the crossroads of two major interstate highways and has several railroads, as well as an international airport that ranks among the country's busiest.

The true catalyst for the explosive growth of Charlotte arrived in the early 1880s when the town's first textile mills were constructed. Born initially from the marriage of Northern capital to the transportation advantages and abundant labor of the region, this new industry thrived and quickly became the economic engine of the Carolina Piedmont. The proximity of the nation's premier cotton-producing region to Charlotte's rail lines soon made the city the center of Carolina textile production. In 1880, Charlotte was home to just over 7,000 people. By 1930, fueled by the ever-growing Southern textile business, the town had blossomed into a city of over 82,000.

As the twentieth century approached, the Southern textile boom created labor and housing demands that were met by the earliest suburbs that rose out of the farms and pastures surrounding the small town. Local businessmen, some of whom had taken full advantage of the region's textile economy, began to address the housing needs of both the new breed of the Southern professional that was emerging, as well as the incoming tide of new arrivals from the surrounding countryside drawn by the lure of textile jobs and mill housing. Charlotte was rapidly outgrowing its four wards, and was for the first time feeling the growing pains of an expanding city.

During the 1890s, the development patterns of Charlotte were influenced by forces still being felt to the present day. The city greeted the arrival of the streetcar, which allowed housing, jobs, churches, and shops to be located farther apart from each other, and walking distance became meaningless. New housing began to break out of the grid mold as the city's first suburbs appeared in the surrounding farm fields and pastures. Charlotte was experiencing the birth of its first suburbs, and the face of the still-young city would change forever.

Dilworth was the first of these suburbs, connected to the town center by the city's maiden electric streetcar line. More new communities quickly followed. Some, such as Myers Park and Elizabeth, have remained strong throughout their history. North Charlotte, Belmont, and others have changed under economic and social challenges. Still others, such as Brooklyn, are gone. Some still cope with seemingly insurmountable pressures, and yet are discovering the key to their future in the strengths of their past.

These photographs and vignettes can give but a glimpse of the history of Charlotte and its neighborhoods. Since the city's beginning as the namesake of England's Queen Charlotte of Mecklenburg, its citizens have strived to maintain a reputation worthy of the Queen City. People here have endured events that they knew were turning points in their history, such as the Civil War. The sweeping impact of other moments in Charlotte's past, such as the beginning and the end of the streetcar system, became evident only in retrospect. Through it all, Charlotte has kept its eye firmly toward its future, sometimes at the expense of those places and things that connect it to the past.

This short work is intended to give a sense of the evolution of Charlotte through the eyes of those who documented the city through photography, with an emphasis on the places where the citizens of the Queen City lived and worked, worshiped and played. Some neighborhoods have benefited from a bounty of early pictures, while others suffer from a lack of attention from the camera. Some of these photographs have been published before, while others make their appearance in public here for the first time. In all, we hope to give the reader a taste of how Charlotte came to be as we know it today, and an idea of the forces that will carry it forward into the future.

John and Amy Rogers
September 1996

One
Downtown:
The Early Days

Since Charlotte's earliest days, the intersection of Trade and Tryon Streets has been the commercial center of the city. This photograph, dating from the 1890s, shows this intersection, known as the Square, as the city stood on the verge of a growth boom fueled by the burgeoning cotton economy and the vision of such business leaders as Edward Dilworth Latta, D.A. Tompkins, and James B. Duke. By the turn of the century, the city's first suburbs would be under construction and horse-drawn trolleys would be yielding to electric streetcars.

The Square is now surrounded by skyscrapers, and cars and buses compete with pedestrians for the street, yet it remains the center of Charlotte's identity—the place where the past and the future vie for our attention. (Robinson-Spangler Carolina Room, Public Library of Charlotte and Mecklenburg County)

Settlers Cemetery, located in Fourth Ward behind the First Presbyterian Church, was Charlotte's main public burial ground until the Civil War era. Many of early Charlotte's most prominent citizens are buried here, most notably the town's first settler, Thomas Polk. Settlers Cemetery eventually closed after the city opened the much larger Elmwood Cemetery in the early 1850s, several blocks to the west. Today Settlers Cemetery is a public park. (Robinson-Spangler Carolina Room, Public Library of Charlotte and Mecklenburg County)

The courthouse that stood at West Trade and North Church Streets was the location of much commerce and communication when this antique photograph was taken. Several courthouses have served the Queen City in its history. From the original structure at the crossroads of Trade and Tryon Streets to today's modern edifice on East Fourth Street, each of Charlotte's courthouses has had its own distinct personality. (Robinson-Spangler Carolina Room, Public Library of Charlotte and Mecklenburg County)

In 1908, Charlotte hosted the annual meeting of the Southern Newspaper Publishers Association. It was held on May 20, the anniversary of the signing of the Mecklenburg Declaration of Independence in 1775. To commemorate the occasion, Major J.C. Hemphill, editor of the Charleston (S.C.) *News and Courier*, and J.P. Caldwell, editor of *The Charlotte Observer*, posed for this photograph. The two men are standing on a plaque that marked the site of the original courthouse at the Square, where local history tells us the declaration was signed. (Robinson-Spangler Carolina Room, Public Library of Charlotte and Mecklenburg County)

Taken in 1924, this photograph shows a Tryon Street that is almost unrecognizable today. In the center of the image is the Independence Building, built in 1908 and noted as North Carolina's first steel-frame skyscraper. The Independence Building, which for years stood as the focal point of the Square, was imploded in 1981. The brick median in this image contains the streetcar rails, and the curbs are lined with early automobiles. The five-globe street lights are low to the sidewalks, designed to aid evening pedestrians rather than motor traffic. (Duke Power Archives)

Imagine arriving in Charlotte by train in the 1840s. A horse-drawn buggy carried travelers to the Central Hotel, where as guests of the hotel they attended important events held in the grand ballroom. In 1887, horse-drawn trolleys were put into service, and were even incorporated into the engraving on the hotel's stationery. In the 1930s, the landmark hotel that stood on the Square was demolished. (North Carolina Collection, University of North Carolina Library at Chapel Hill)

These stylish residents of Charlotte are enjoying an outing in their Cadillac automobile around 1907. They're motoring past the First Presbyterian Church, one of the city's most enduring landmarks. No one is certain of their names, but the notes made on the back of this antique photograph indicate that Edw. Robbins, Flora Bryant, Mrs. Frank Caldwell Alexander (Dr. Charles' daughter), and Mrs. Floyd Summer (?) are shown. First Presbyterian, a Gothic Revival-style church, evolved in stages, with the entrance dating from 1857, the steeple from 1884, and the present sanctuary from 1895. Its campus continues to occupy an entire city block, although there have been four major building expansions in the twentieth century. The church remains a religious focal point of this heavily Presbyterian city. (North Carolina Collection, University of North Carolina Library at Chapel Hill)

ailroads, and Charlotte's position as a transportation crossroads, were certainly assets to the rea's economic growth in the late nineteenth and early twentieth centuries. Railroads that erved Charlotte included the Carolina Central, the Richmond & Danville, and the Seaboard Airline. The freight and passenger services the railroads provided to Charlotte played a key role n the city's development as a textile center. Here, a steam engine departs Charlotte's Southern Railroad depot. (Robinson-Spangler Carolina Room, Public Library of Charlotte and Mecklenburg County)

ulia M. Alexander was Charlotte's first female lawyer, and this 1925 photograph depicts her South Tryon Street campaign headquarters hung with a banner promoting Alexander's campaign for mayor. Note the way in which these classically designed buildings, each with its own distinct personality, came together to form a streetscape that clearly defined Charlotte's central business district. (Robinson-Spangler Carolina Room, Public Library of Charlotte and Mecklenburg County)

Mayor T.L. Kirkpatrick and the city's board of aldermen posed on the steps of Charlotte City Hall in January of 1916. This Romanesque-style building from 1891 stood at the corner of North Tryon and Fifth Streets. (Robinson-Spangler Carolina Room, Public Library of Charlotte and Mecklenburg County)

The seeds of Charlotte's successful future can be seen clearly in this early 1900s photograph taken from Tompkins Tower. The dome of the city's courthouse appears at the right of the view, and the cluster of buildings that constitute the thriving downtown business district already foretell of the prosperity the young city would grow to achieve. (Robinson-Spangler Carolina Room, Public Library of Charlotte and Mecklenburg County)

Unpaved streets and open-air stores are what people remember about Charlotte's early days at the turn of the century. Women's long skirts and high-button shoes and men's "dusters" kept out the grit and grime of the young city. This photograph, taken in front of the corner store at East Trade and North Brevard Streets, dates from c. 1910. (Robinson-Spangler Carolina Room, Public Library of Charlotte and Mecklenburg County)

As in most cities, the town center served not only as the business core, but also as the location of the best shopping, whether the store was large or small. Most of Charlotte's downtown retail establishments were operated as sole proprietorships, such as Brockman's Book Store at 210 South Tryon Street. This photograph of Brockman's interior, taken during World War I, shows Camp Greene pennants for sale along with those for Charlotte High School. (Robinson-Spangler Carolina Room, Public Library of Charlotte and Mecklenburg County)

The Ford Motor Company has had a long association with Charlotte. A Ford assembly plant operated here from 1915 until the 1930s. This Ford garage, located in the 200 block of North College Street, is believed to have been the first Ford repair shop in the city. It was operated by Doc Crowell and W.G. Frye. Note the early three-digit telephone number lettered on the storefront. (Robinson-Spangler Carolina Room, Public Library of Charlotte and Mecklenburg County)

Salesmen from the Mecklenburg Auto Company show off their merchandise in 1911. The showroom was located at 211 South Church Street, on the edge of the Third Ward neighborhood. (Robinson-Spangler Carolina Room, Public Library of Charlotte and Mecklenburg County)

Thad Tate's immaculately appointed barber shop was located just one block away from the Square on East Fourth Street, between Tryon and College Streets. With its stamped-tin ceiling and modern features, the shop was staffed by blacks but served only white customers. Other barber shops within the city's black communities provided services to their neighborhood patrons. This photograph was taken during the 1930s. (Second Ward High School National Alumni Foundation)

This commanding structure served as Charlotte's post office from 1881 until 1915. It stood on West Trade Street, where it shared the block with the United States Mint building, visible at the right of the photograph. The post office was demolished in 1915, and replaced with a new building, which eventually became too small to meet the city's needs. The post office building was then expanded, and the mint building was moved to its present home in the Eastover neighborhood, where it began its new life as the city's art museum. (North Carolina Collection, University of North Carolina Library at Chapel Hill)

Charlotte has always dressed up the streets for special events. This commemorative arch, built over the trolley line and illuminated for night viewing, was erected for President William Howard Taft's 1909 visit to Charlotte. (Duke Power Archives)

William Henry Belk opened the first Belk department store in 1895, near the corner of Trade and Tryon Streets. As the store grew, it took over more and more storefronts on both streets, as evidenced in this group photograph of Belk employees taken in the 1920s in front of the store's Trade Street entrance. Today, Belk's is one of the major department store chains in the Southeast, and is still headquartered in the Queen City under the leadership of the Belk family. (Robinson-Spangler Carolina Room, Public Library of Charlotte and Mecklenburg County)

D.A. Tompkins is remembered for his vision for Charlotte's future, and for the energy he brought to the Queen City. Believing in the power of the South's tremendous resources, he became one of the region's driving forces in its development as a successful textile center. (Charlotte Historic District Commission)

A blanket of snow covers Tryon Street near the Square in this 1926 photograph. In the early days, when Charlotte was smaller and still had a streetcar system in place, transportation was easier when the city suffered one of its occasional "blizzards." Today a snowstorm, even one that brings only a few inches, can bring the city almost to a standstill—especially at night. (Duke Power Archives)

This view, looking northeast on Tryon Street, shows two of the last surviving commercial buildings from the downtown's early days. Even then, as center-city streets became busier with each year's growth, pedestrian safety was a strong concern. The banner above the moving vehicles in the background of this 1930s-era image reads, "Look, live, don't die!" (Duke Power Archives)

Every imaginable sort of street traffic—pedestrian, streetcar, automobile, bicycle—shared the road in Charlotte's early days. This photograph was taken looking down the first block of East Trade Street toward Tryon Street. Just to the left of the power pole in the center of the image is Kings Business College, shown here in its original location before its move to the Elizabeth neighborhood. (Robinson-Spangler Carolina Room, Public Library of Charlotte and Mecklenburg County)

The Selwyn

Charlotte, N.C.

Hon E. L. Baxter Davidson
City

What could have been so urgent that a Selwyn Hotel guest paid 10¢ to post a special delivery letter to the Davidson family household? The hotel's stationery bore an engraved image that depicted not only the building's architectural details, but also the fine automobiles that wheeled by. The name of the recipient and "city" was enough information on a letter in the days when a postal carrier knew every family on his route. No return address was needed either—everyone knew where the Selwyn was. (North Carolina Collection, University of North Carolina Library at Chapel Hill)

The Selwyn, built in 1907, was considered Charlotte's first modern hotel. It occupied the corner of West Trade Street, across from First Presbyterian Church and only one block from the Square. The hotel operated continuously until its closing in 1960. In this photograph, power company linemen work on the service lines to the hotel. (Duke Power Archives)

n its heyday as Charlotte's business and retail center, Tryon Street was decked out for the holidays. "Christmas Greetings" flashed the festooned lights of this Belk Brothers department store display that also brightly proclaimed the year—1931—in a star at the center. (Duke Power Archives)

This view of the Square, captured in December of 1937, shows busy holiday shoppers sharing the street with Charlotte's streetcars for the last time. Trolley service ended the following year. None of the buildings shown in this photograph remain today. (Duke Power Archives)

Two
The Four Wards:
Charlotte's First Neighborhoods

he division of Charlotte into four wards was a natural progression from the city's birth as a
rossroads. The convergence of Trade and Tryon Streets, which had long existed as trading
aths, created four distinct neighborhoods, each with its own personality. Along these streets,
nd on the parallel avenues, grand residences like the one shown here were common,
xhibiting the ornate woodwork and turn-of-the-century details typical of the Victorian style.

Fourth Ward would always retain some of its residential character, even in its most difficult
ays, while its sister wards would each undergo dramatic changes. Today, many of the best
xamples of Charlotte's Victorian-era residences survive in Fourth Ward, or in isolation within
ther early neighborhoods. (North Carolina Collection, University of North Carolina Library
t Chapel Hill)

Charlotte's four wards each contained an elementary school for white children, and all bu
Third Ward had schools that served the black community. The photograph above, taken in
1918, shows the sixth grade class posing at the wood-frame Myers Street School in Second
Ward. Below is the First Ward Graded School, which was attended by that neighborhood's
white children. (Robinson-Spangler Carolina Room, Public Library of Charlotte and
Mecklenburg County)

=THE=

AFRO-AMERICAN MUTUAL

INSURANCE COMPANY

CHARLOTTE, N. C.

OFFICERS

J. T. WILLIAMS	T. L. TATE	S. B. WASHINGTON	J. W. CROCKETT
President	Vice-President	Treasurer	Secretary and General Manager

P. O. BOX 586   227 E. TRADE ST.

AGENTS WANTED   **AGENTS WANTED**

oth the Afro-American Mutual Insurance Company and the Southern Fidelity Mutual nsurance Company featured their services to the black community in advertisements during he 1930s and '40s. Afro-American Mutual had an office on East Trade Street, a convenient ocation for its clientele in the adjacent First and Second Ward neighborhoods. The company's fficers are listed in the advertisement above. President J.T. Williams' home, adorned with ntricate trim and dozens of turned balusters along its wide front porch, stood unchanged for ecades on South Brevard Street. It fell victim to urban renewal in the 1970s. (Second Ward ligh School National Alumni Foundation)

This fine house belonged to the William Yongue family. Granddaughter Mildred Mosle remembers, "We lived right around the corner. All my granddaddy's children lived aroune him." The house, located on East Eighth Street in First Ward, proudly displays the Victoriar architectural details that were popular at the time the photograph was taken, around 1910 (Second Ward High School National Alumni Foundation)

The Hotel Alexander, situated in Third Ward at the corner of North McDowell and East Nintr Streets, was for many years the only hotel that accommodated blacks traveling to and through Charlotte. The three-story building also contained a coffee shop. (Second Ward High Schoo National Alumni Association)

The Diamond family posed for a casual portrait in 1937, as America continued to brave the Depression years. This photograph of youngsters Vermelle and Kenneth Jr., along with their parents, Cora and Kenneth Diamond Sr., was featured in an advertisement that promoted insurance. An adult could be insured against hospital expenses for 75¢ per month; for each child the premium was 25¢. (Second Ward High School National Alumni Foundation)

The First United Presbyterian Church, located in First Ward at the corner of North College and East Seventh Streets, was built in 1893. This church, which is still used by its original congregation, was one of the most prosperous in its neighborhood. Note the homes along North College Street captured in this 1950s photograph; although the church remains, the houses are gone. (Kugler's Studio)

Some of Charlotte's in-town streets remained unpaved into the late 1940s. Here is East Sixth Street at its intersection with North Davidson Street. This section of First Ward vanished through urban renewal in subsequent years, and the area shown here became part of Earle Village, downtown Charlotte's largest low-rise public housing project. (Robinson-Spangler Carolina Room, Public Library of Charlotte and Mecklenburg County)

ew families in Charlotte achieved the rominence of the Alexander family. hown in this photograph are echariah Jr. (seated), Frederick (left), ouis (center), and Kelly Sr. A fifth rother, Isaac, died while still a eenager. The four surviving sons of echariah Alexander Sr. and his wife ouise were successful businessmen, but hey are perhaps best known for romoting civil rights and other issues rucial to the survival of the black ommunity. (Second Ward High chool National Alumni Foundation)

ompare the family group portrait bove with the one shown here. Fred lexander (in the far left in the hotograph above) is now State enator Fred Alexander, the first black o be elected to North Carolina's state enate since Reconstruction. (Second ʼard High School National Alumni oundation)

Most of the Victorian-style homes in Charlotte's four wards were made of wood, and used brick or stone only for the foundations and chimneys. This, the First Ward residence of businessman Thad L. Tate, was unusual. The turn-of-the-century home at 504 East Seventh Street was built of solid brick and complemented by elaborate, carved wood trim. In this fashion, it bridged the gap between true Victorian architecture of the late nineteenth century and the newer, more down-to-earth bungalow style that was gaining popularity in the twentieth. (*The Charlotte Observer*)

Its full name is the Mecklenburg Investment Company Building, but people familiar with its history and importance often refer to it just as "M.I.C." In 1921, the South Brevard Street structure represented the realization of a dream for the black business community—its own building to house offices and meeting space. The three-story building survives today with few changes to its original design. (Second Ward High School National Alumni Foundation)

ook beyond the weathering of these extremely rare photographs to see Sarah Hampton Diamond at the reins (above), and her husband Jim with the family's pet bulldogs, Jake and Monk (below). Sarah was licensed in 1914 by the City of Charlotte to operate a dray, or horse-drawn cart, but it was Jim who most often drove the dray. He was even granted a special license to deliver opium from the local pharmacies. The Diamonds' granddaughter remembers that her granddaddy once got a ticket while driving his dray through the Square downtown. Jim had exceeded the speed limit: it was 5 miles per hour. (Second Ward High School National Alumni Foundation)

It's May 17, 1928, at Second Ward School, the first public high school for blacks in Charlotte Mecklenburg. The students, many of whom lived across town in black neighborhoods such a Biddleville and Washington Heights, walked several miles to school each day. Back then, th school offered instruction only through the eighth grade. Students seeking further educatio had to seek it elsewhere, and many went on to Johnson C. Smith University, which had a hig school division as well as college programs. By the 1940s, Second Ward provided instruction fo students through the twelfth grade. The school graduated its last class in 1969. (Second War High School National Alumni Foundation)

Mildred Mosley remembers when this 1944 portrait of Second Ward's basketball team wa taken. The two young women are probably cheerleaders, most likely Flossie Gantt and Norm Holden, but no one has been able to identify the child peeking through the shadowy window o the right. (Second Ward High School National Alumni Foundation)

The long-standing football rivalry between the West Charlotte and Second Ward high schools played itself out every year at the Queen City Classic football game. Started in 1947, the annual event boasted its own parade, and in 1948 the first Miss Queen City Classic was crowned. This portrait captures a smiling Vermelle Diamond, Miss Queen City Classic of 1949, her arms full of flowers and surrounded by well-wishers. (Second Ward High School National Alumni Foundation)

This aerial photograph shows the Brooklyn neighborhood just prior to its "redevelopment."
Stonewall Street, becoming West Independence Boulevard, is the prominent artery runnin
from left to right across the photograph. Second Ward School lies at the right of the pictur
East Trade Street is identifiable near the top, with the old Mecklenburg County Courthous
and Charlotte City Hall still recognizable. Brooklyn, as Second Ward came to be known, wa

...ne of Charlotte's most vibrant neighborhoods until its destruction in the name of urban ...newal. As this photograph shows, the area offered its residents a dense mixture of housing, ...mployment, shopping, and social opportunities, and was a center of the city's African-...merican community. The houses and businesses in the foreground were obliterated by the ...evelopment of the John Belk Freeway. (Charlotte Historic District Commission)

Sunflowers bloom in this 1959 urban portrait of Long Street, once part of the Brooklyn neighborhood. Many areas that provided housing for families of modest means were in their own ways self-sufficient. They contained schools, churches, and stores—such as Teague's Place, visible here just below the spire of the Covenant Presbyterian Church. Long Street vanished when the Brooklyn structures were leveled and residents relocated to other neighborhoods during a phase of intense urban renewal. (The Charlotte Observer)

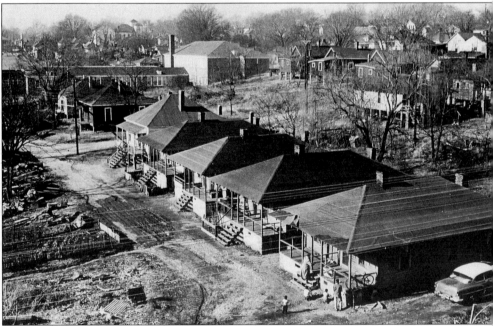

Charlotte's urban renewal movement in the 1970s radically changed the face of the city' economically depressed neighborhoods. The families who lived in the houses seen in this earl 1960s photograph recognized the complexities of a growing city and the need for change, bu many of the residents of the old Brooklyn community still reminisce about the days whei everything was within walking distance and friends could talk to each other over their porcl rails. (*The Charlotte Observer*)

This more recent photograph shows Second Ward School as it appeared after World War II. It was the campus of Carver College and offered a two-year college program for black students. Since Second Ward School was still in use as a high school, the college students attended their classes in the late afternoon and evening hours. Carver College later became part of the Central Piedmont Community College. (Robinson-Spangler Carolina Room, Public Library of Charlotte and Mecklenburg County)

Although taken to document the installation of new electrical transmission lines, this early 1930s photograph also captured a rare view of Charlotte's more modest housing from that era. The backs of these homes face Sugar Creek at its crossing with Fourth Street. This densely built neighborhood would slowly decline until it was cleared over three decades later as part of the redevelopment of Second Ward. (Duke Power Archives)

In this unusual image, the strut of an airplane's wing parallels Tryon Street and frames the Third Ward neighborhood at the bottom of the photograph. The year was 1944, and residences still lined Third Ward's streets, an area now occupied by offices and parking lots. Church Street, which bisects this picture, has changed as much as Tryon Street since this photograph was taken. At the top of the image lies Fourth Ward, with its tree-lined streets. (Duke Power Archives)

Considered to be the first private hospital in the United States developed for black patients Good Samaritan Hospital stood on South Mint Street in the Third Ward neighborhood. It wa built in 1888 by the Charlotte Episcopal congregation. Spearheading much of the effort wa Jane Wilkes, the wife of John Wilkes, the owner of Mecklenburg Iron Works. Mrs. Wilkes wa also instrumental in the establishment of St. Peter's Home and Hospital, which opened in 187 in nearby Fourth Ward. St. Peter's has been remodeled and transformed into residentia condominiums. Good Samaritan Hospital is gone. (*The Charlotte Observer*)

Few Charlotte residents experienced as much notoriety in the era after the Civil War as the widow of Confederate General Thomas A. "Stonewall" Jackson. Mary Anna Morrison Jackson returned to her native Charlotte after her husband died from complications after losing an arm at Chancellorsville in May of 1863. (Robinson-Spangler Carolina Room, Public Library of Charlotte and Mecklenburg County)

Mrs. Stonewall Jackson's Residence Charlotte N C

The Jackson House, which stood in the 300 block of West Trade Street, was featured on Charlotte postcards of the era. Mrs. Jackson often presided over Confederate Veterans' Day and other functions until her death in 1915. (North Carolina Collection, University of North Carolina Library at Chapel Hill)

This 1950s view of North Graham Street, taken looking south toward West Tenth Street shows the street's long history as an important thoroughfare along the side of Fourth Ward. With its designation as part of the North Carolina highway system, North Graham Street was a heavily traveled artery, and for decades it delineated the edge of Fourth Ward. Although the area declined after the 1950s, today new residents are drawn to the revitalized Fourth Ward neighborhood. Graham Street has slowly been reclaiming some of its earlier character as an avenue that mixes both residential and small business uses. (Robinson-Spangler Carolina Room, Public Library of Charlotte and Mecklenburg County)

Low- to mid-rise apartment buildings have always been an important feature of Charlotte's housing profile. Not only were they built in many of the city's newer neighborhoods beginning in the 1920s, but they were also found in the center city, most notably in Fourth Ward. A number of these buildings appeared along North Church Street in the 1920s and 1930s. The Jefferson, shown here in its early days, as well as the Frederick, the Poplar, and others provided housing for the families employed by the shops and offices on nearby Tryon Street. (Duke Power Archives)

The Manger Inn was considered one of downtown Charlotte's first "modern" hotels. It was an instant success with traveling businessmen. Facing the 600 block of North Tryon Street, the Manger Inn sat immediately adjacent to Fourth Ward. This photograph, with the Poplar Street Apartments at the top, shows many of the Fourth Ward residences that were removed as part of the neighborhood revitalization plan of the 1970s. (Kugler's Studio)

Look at these beauties! It's 1956, and a new car would set you back about $2,000, less for a used car. Take your pick from any of these on display at "The Auto Wheel," Frank Woods' South Mint Street car dealership in Third Ward. The success of this business was due in part to its visibility, as the cars were seen by all who drove or walked along this busy street. Judging from the styles shown in this photograph, two-toned paint was popular. (Kugler's Studio)

The carved marble monument in the foreground of this image bears the family name Morehead. Beyond it, and throughout Elmwood Cemetery, memorials stand in tribute to many of Charlotte's founders and prominent benefactors. Among the familiar names are Myers, Latta, Belk, McNinch, Springs, Dillard, McAden, Pegram, Cole, Severs, Cannon, and Tate. There is also a monument to the area's Confederate soldiers. With the end of segregation, the fence that separated Elmwood from the adjoining Pinewood Cemetery was removed. Tucked into an area bordered by Third Ward, Fourth Ward, and the edge of Greenville, the cemetery remains a peaceful enclave. Today, Charlotte's skyline of bold modern buildings, visible just a few blocks south of the cemetery, are an interesting visual contrast to the calm atmosphere of Elmwood Cemetery. (John Reynolds Rogers Jr.)

It's easy to forget how much old-style neighborhoods had to offer their residents. When the Berryhill House was built on West Ninth Street, almost everything a family could need was within walking distance; the Berryhill Grocery was just across the street. This photograph of the home's entrance shows the elaborate handmade brackets that decorate the porch and eaves of the Fourth Ward house. (John Reynolds Rogers Jr.).

Three
Dilworth and Wilmore:
The Streetcar's New Direction

Few events have had as powerful an impact on the history of Charlotte as the arrival of the electric streetcar. Although Charlotte had horse-drawn trolleys on Trade and Tryon Streets, it was Edward Dilworth Latta's electric trolley that allowed the city to expand outside the confines of the four wards. Not only did Latta's Dilworth neighborhood introduce the suburb to Charlotte, it eliminated walking distance between work and home as a factor in choosing where to live.

Latta's Charlotte Street Railway Company began operation in May of 1891, and was replaced five years later by the Charlotte Electric Railway. The electric trolley, with its "moving billboard" proclaiming "Buy a home in Dilworth for rent money," made the development of Dilworth and neighboring Wilmore possible. (Robinson-Spangler Carolina Room, Public Library of Charlotte and Mecklenburg County)

No home in Dilworth was grander than the residence of namesake businessman Edward Dilworth Latta himself. Constructed in the 600 block of East Boulevard, the home's eclectic mix of classical and modern architectural elements reflected Latta's many interests. The house, adjacent to the Holy Trinity Greek Orthodox Church, was demolished and a new structure was built on its site to accommodate the educational and recreational activities of the growing church. (Charlotte Historic District Commission)

The Southern Public Utilities Company was an early subsidiary of what is now the Duke Power Company. This portrait, taken in March of 1935, shows a group of the company's linemen posing near Dilworth. The electrification of the streetcar system, as well as the new electrical appliances and other conveniences made available through electric companies, helped make Charlotte's early suburbs the great successes they were. (Duke Power Archives)

The older sections of the Dilworth neighborhood featured areas of rolling terrain, which enabled the Charlotte Consolidated Construction Company to develop Latta Park, with its natural vistas. Others used this feature of the new neighborhood to their advantage as well, such as this group of children playing in a backyard on Rensselaer Avenue around 1900. (Robinson-Spangler Carolina Room, Public Library of Charlotte and Mecklenburg County)

The arrival of the textile mills in Charlotte had an economic impact on the city that would be unrivaled until the explosive growth of the banking industry almost a century later. The mills provided a large employment base and created numerous support industries. One of the results of this rapid development was a boom in neighborhood building as Charlotte's population swelled from just over 7,000 in 1880 to more than 82,000 in 1930, the year this photograph was taken. These women are posing at their machines in the 1893 Atherton Mill, situated between the Dilworth and Wilmore neighborhoods. The factory that employed the workers seen here now serves as the centerpiece of the fashionable South End district, a redevelopment project that features antique shops, restaurants, and offices. (Duke Power Archives)

Its name was too long for casual conversation—"The Charlotte Consolidated Construction Company"—so people just called it "the 4Cs." Made up of a group of the area's best-known businessmen under the leadership of Edward Dilworth Latta, the "4Cs" developed Latta Park and its pavilion, shown here. Offering far more than just gardens and natural areas, Latta Park became the city's major amusement park after its opening in 1891. It offered boating, concerts, races, picnics, games, and greenhouses—and visitors could reach it all by trolley. Although in later years the lake was drained and sections of the park were developed as part of a growing Dilworth, today Latta Park remains one of Charlotte's favorite neighborhood parks. (North Carolina Collection, University of North Carolina Library at Chapel Hill)

The first of Charlotte's parks to be connected to the city by the streetcar line in the 1890s, Latta Park still remains at its original location in the Dilworth neighborhood. The lake pictured here was once large enough to accommodate boaters, but a dam built in recent years now controls the lake's flow to a trickling stream that winds its way through the park. (Charlotte Historic District Commission)

"It is genuine. It is a veritable kindergarten of history, teaching equestrianism, primitive savagery and civil military tactics." So read a section of the exhaustive advertisement for Buffalo Bill Cody's Wild West Show printed in October 1901. Charlotte was a young town at the turn of the century, but already beginning to attract touring entertainers. Held at the exposition grounds in what would later become part of the Dilworth neighborhood, its organizers promised that the show would be "more complete than ever, if such a thing were possible." (North Carolina Collection, University of North Carolina Library at Chapel Hill)

Here is an interesting turn-of-the-century composite photograph offering two different views of Latta Park in Dilworth. The small inset photograph shows the tranquil lake with its boathouse steps leading to a waiting canoe, while the larger photograph depicts the excitement of a crowd gathered in the grandstand to watch an afternoon horse race. (Charlotte Historic District Commission)

Charlotte's reputation for almost constant modernization is not a recent phenomenon. When the city's public transportation evolved from trolleys to buses in the late 1930s, the old trolley barn was converted to accommodate the new equipment. These 1938 photographs show the removal of the trolley barn's classical, arched facade (above) and the proud, modern replacement, almost stark by contrast (below). (Duke Power Archives)

'In 1861, Jewish women from Charlotte raised $150 to 'assist Confederate volunteers,'" wrote Morris Speizman in his book, *The Jews of Charlotte*. From early shopkeeper Samuel Wittkowsky to modern-day philanthropist I.D. Blumenthal, Jews have long played a part in Charlotte's social, economic, and political history. In this interesting photograph of Temple Israel, candles on a Chanukah menorah burn to celebrate the Jewish Festival of Lights. The Dilworth Road Temple was demolished in the 1990s to allow for residential in-fill development, and the congregation relocated to a new facility at Shalom Park. (*The Charlotte Observer*)

Although popular in the downtown area and in other early Charlotte suburbs, this building type was unusual in Dilworth. The twelve-unit apartment building, built by Charlotte developer John Crosland, stood on what is now part of the campus of the Covenant Presbyterian Church at the intersection of Dilworth Road and Arosa Avenue. The Gothic-Tudor style illustrated here was fashionable in Charlotte during the period between the two world wars, when these apartments were built. (Duke Power Archives)

By the late 1940s, South Boulevard had lost its identity as the entrance boulevard to Dilworth. This view of South Boulevard was taken looking south from its intersection with Bland Street, away from the downtown area. Just past the intersection, to the right, stands the Duke Power Company's bus barn, which formerly served as the trolley barn. The boulevard's houses have long since vanished in the face of commercial redevelopment. (Robinson-Spangler Carolina Room, Public Library of Charlotte and Mecklenburg County)

The intersection of Morehead Street and Dilworth Road, shown here in 1950, became to many Charlotteans the entrance to Dilworth after the 1911 expansion plan was fulfilled. One of the neighborhood's landmark churches, Covenant Presbyterian, which now dominates this intersection, had yet to be built when this photograph was taken. (Robinson-Spangler Carolina Room, Public Library of Charlotte and Mecklenburg County)

52

The Morehead Street corridor has undergone many changes in character throughout its history, as this early 1960s photograph can attest. This Shoney's restaurant, now gone, brought the convenience and contemporary design of the 1960s to the edge of Dilworth. The familiar spire of the Covenant Presbyterian Church can be seen in the distance. (Kugler's Studio)

Everyone loves a parade and Charlotteans are no exception. Here, the annual Carolinas Carousel parade travels down East Boulevard. The Gothic Revival-style twin towers of the Dilworth United Methodist Church can be seen behind the Queen City Coach "Arabian Nights" parade float. (Kugler's Studio)

The original Nebel Knitting Mill building with its classic, turn-of-the-century mill architecture, faced a fate similar to that of other textile mills upon closing. Luckily, the contributions of the Nebel Mill to the architectural and social history of Charlotte were recognized, and the building is now listed on the National Register of Historic Places. It was remodeled in the 1990s and now houses a restaurant and offices. (John Reynolds Rogers Jr.)

Compare this entrance to the Nebel Knitting Mill's annex with the window lintel from the original building above. The Art Moderne addition was built in the 1920s, and although it adjoins the recently rehabilitated original mill, it still awaits renovation. (John Reynolds Rogers Jr.)

Although the front entrance to the Greater Galilee Baptist Church has been obscured by the addition of awnings that over its walkway, this side view shows many of the building's Gothic Revival-style details. The church is situated on West Park Avenue in the Wilmore neighborhood, surrounded by a cluster of small homes. (John Reynolds Rogers Jr.)

The Nebel Knitting Mill produced hosiery and other knitwear from its location between the Dilworth and Wilmore communities. For decades, Nebel provided employment to many residents of both neighborhoods. This 1930s-era promotional photograph was produced by the Duke Power Company to tout the advantages of adequate electric lighting in a manufacturing setting. (Duke Power Archives)

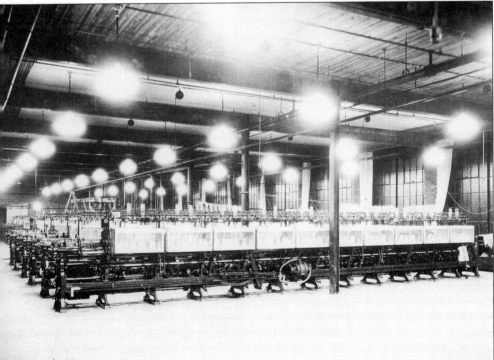

The sign is new but the neighborhood is old. "Wilmore–1914." Just to the west and across the railroad tracks from Dilworth, Wilmore shares many similarities with its better-known older neighbor. Both contain a mixture of housing styles. This two-story, four-unit dwelling on Wilmore's Cliffwood Place is a good example of the style of architecture found on both the east and west sides of the streets the neighborhoods share. (John Reynolds Rogers Jr.)

This well-tended Wilmore home enjoys a view of Cliffwood Place from atop the hill that inspired the street's name. The neighborhood's road design mirrors that of Dilworth: a basic grid pattern with some curved streets that follow natural topography. Missing in this small neighborhood is a park, but Wilmore residents can easily walk down West Park Avenue, cross South Boulevard, and travel along East Park Avenue to reach Latta Park in Dilworth just a short distance away. (John Reynolds Rogers Jr.)

Four
Cherry, Myers Park, and Eastover:
Room to Grow

The Ardsley Road shown in this photograph bears little resemblance to the tree-lined street that runs through the heart of Myers Park today. Development of the new suburb began in 1911 under the leadership of George Stephens. To transform the farmland owned by the Myers family, Stephens called on some of the nation's best designers to create Myers Park, which would adjoin the already established Cherry neighborhood. Much of the area grew incrementally. The earliest residence on the street, at no. 801, was built in 1915 by C.I. Buckholder. The oaks that form the shady canopy over much of the neighborhood can be seen here as new saplings.

The construction of Eastover, one of the first suburbs designed for access by automobiles rather than streetcars, followed in 1927. Developed by the E.C. Griffith Company, it would reflect much of the character of neighboring Myers Park with its curvilinear streets and stately homes. (Robinson-Spangler Carolina Room, Public Library of Charlotte and Mecklenburg County)

The Stephens Company commissioned this 1912 aerial view of Myers Park's overall design as a way to promote the new neighborhood. The intricate street layout was the work of Boston designer John Nolen, who conceived this plan early in his career and went on to become one of the premier urban designers of his day. The incorporation of natural contours and the designation of land for parks and other open spaces were hallmarks of Nolen's work. In this view, the location of Myers Park relative to downtown, as well as the earlier suburbs such as Dilworth and Elizabeth, can be seen. Even Kings Mountain and Spencer Mountain appear in the distant background. (North Carolina Collection, University of North Carolina Library at Chapel Hill)

Myers Park developed very quickly in its early years. Here, workers labor to create streets and sidewalks as the already operational streetcar passes by. In the background, new homes claim their places in what had been farmland just a few short years before. The Stephens Company worked to complete each phase of the street layout quickly, believing that finished streets and sidewalks helped the sale of house lots remain strong. Even the young trees just beginning to spread their roots were part of designer John Nolen's overall plan for the neighborhood. (Robinson-Spangler Carolina Room, Public Library of Charlotte and Mecklenburg County)

was all part of the vision of neighborhood planners John Nolen and Earle Sumner Draper. Once the Stephens Company began in earnest to develop Myers Park, the new neighborhood boomed. The top photograph shows a portion of Myers Park with its houses and streets under construction simultaneously. The bottom photograph depicts three recently completed homes on Hermitage Road at Queens Road, standing proudly among the new streets, sidewalks, trolley tracks, and street lights. (Robinson-Spangler Carolina Room, Public Library of Charlotte and Mecklenburg County)

One of Charlotte's best-known residences is the Duke Mansion, known formally as "White Oaks," at 400 Hermitage Road in Myers Park. The house, built in 1915 for Southern Public Utilities president Z.V. Taylor, appeared as shown here until it was bought by utility and tobacco magnate James B. Duke around 1920. Duke commissioned Charlotte architect C.C. Hook to design additions that tripled the home's dimensions to roughly its present size. (Robinson-Spangler Carolina Room, Public Library of Charlotte and Mecklenburg County)

The success of Myers Park was in large part due to the hiring by developer George Stephens of John Nolen, who was just completing his training in landscape architecture at Harvard University. Nolen went on to become one of the nation's most prominent urban designers. Many of Myers Park's most identifiable features are Nolen designs, including this 1912 streetcar station at the intersection of Queens Road and Fourth Street (Randolph Road). Built of granite quarried in Winnsboro, South Carolina, the structure's center section was later removed to accommodate the widening of Queens Road. The side elements still stand today. (Robinson-Spangler Carolina Room, Public Library of Charlotte and Mecklenburg County)

The Myers Park neighborhood as we now know it has evolved dramatically from its early days as farmland. The lush, majestic canopy of oak trees that shade its winding streets today were planted during the area's development in the 1920s and 1930s. Here, a workman walks alongside a wagon delivering new trees—gathered from the surrounding countryside—to the growing neighborhood. (Robinson-Spangler Carolina Room, Public Library of Charlotte and Mecklenburg County)

This view of Queens College shows the school shortly after the completion of its new campus in Myers Park. Begun as the Charlotte Female Institute in 1857, it was located in First Ward at the corner of Ninth and College Streets. The school, later re-christened Presbyterian College, began to outgrow its campus and the Stephens Company donated the new site, pictured here, in Myers Park. The college relocated to this site in 1912, occupying a new campus that was paid for in part by donations made by some of the new neighborhood's earliest residents. Upon its move, the school became known as Queens College, in honor of the city's namesake, Queen Charlotte. (North Carolina Collection, University of North Carolina Library at Chapel Hill)

These early 1900s views of Providence Road show today's major artery when it was a country dirt road. It defined the eastern edge of Myers Park, as shown at the right of the lower illustration. The area on the opposite side of Providence Road would later develop as the Eastover neighborhood. Today, the road serves as the boundary between these two Charlotte communities. (Robinson-Spangler Carolina Room, Public Library of Charlotte and Mecklenburg County)

Few intersections are better known in Charlotte than the intersection of Queens and Providence Roads, where the Myers Park and Eastover neighborhoods meet. In this late 1940s photograph, two of today's landmarks are already visible: the Townhouse Restaurant and the A&P Supermarket. (Robinson-Spangler Carolina Room, Public Library of Charlotte and Mecklenburg County)

has often been said erroneously that the Cherry neighborhood was developed and designed to house the families who worked for affluent homeowners in adjacent Myers Park. But Cherry, mapped in 1891, was established as a working-class suburb at least a decade before Myers Park was developed. Located just half a mile from Brooklyn, Cherry represented the first opportunity for black families to own their own homes, away from the crowded rental housing in the city. Many of the dwellings were duplexes; others were cottages such as the one shown here, shaded by its own towering oak tree. (*The Charlotte Observer*)

With its simple, yet dignified presence, the Mount Zion Lutheran Church on Luther Street has been a landmark in the Cherry neighborhood for one hundred years. The wood-framed house of worship was built when Cherry was new, and was attended by the laborers, farmers, and blacksmiths who came to the young neighborhood from the center city. Although it would be many years before homes here had indoor plumbing, even early Cherry homes offered something a city rental could not—room for a garden. (*The Charlotte Observer*)

63

In 1837, a branch of the United States Mint was established in Charlotte in response to the discovery of gold in the region. The Mint building, shown here, stood at the corner of West Trade and Mint Streets. Until the outbreak of the Civil War, the facility manufactured gold coins, and after the war, it served as an assay office and courthouse and also housed the offices of several civic associations. The building was slated for demolition in 1933 to make way for Charlotte's new federal courthouse, but was spared; instead of being demolished it was dismantled and rebuilt in the Eastover neighborhood as the core structure of the city's Mint Museum of Art. (Robinson-Spangler Carolina Room, Public Library of Charlotte and Mecklenburg County)

It's July 1, 1953, and H.A. Merritt, sales manager at the Duke Power Company, looks over the Soap Box Derby entry constructed by Harry Hawkins of Eastover's Fenton Place. Even though it's a hot, Southern summer day, Merritt sports a hat, coat, necktie, and long-sleeved shirt (Duke Power Archives)

64

This small block of shops—a grocery store, a drugstore, and a hardware store—once anchored this corner of Park Road, near what is now the Park Road Shopping Center. Such small neighborhood service centers were once common in Charlotte, but they have all but vanished in the path of larger shopping developments and rapid suburbanization. (Kugler's Studio)

The Park Road Shopping Center, as it appeared here in its infancy, is almost unrecognizable today. With anchor tenants Woolworth's, Eckerd Drugs, A&P, and Colonial Stores, and a vast parking lot, the center acknowledged the 1950s as the age of the automobile. The wooded residential neighborhood that formed the edge of Myers Park, shown at the top of the photograph, remains, but commercial development now fills both sides of Woodlawn and Park Roads, shown at the bottom. (Kugler's Studio)

One of Charlotte's most popular public parks is Freedom Park. On the edge of Myers Park, this gathering place has played host to the Charlotte Symphony Pops series, the annual Festival in the Park, and other community events. One afternoon in 1954, this park, which was created in honor of the city's World War II armed forces members, saw thousands turn out to hear Dr. Norman Vincent Peale and President Dwight D. Eisenhower. The photograph to the left shows the park in its early days, before the band shell was constructed on the small island in the lake. Below, hundreds worship at a 1961 Easter sunrise service. (Top photograph Kugler's Studio; bottom photograph Robinson-Spangler Carolina Room, Public Library of Charlotte and Mecklenburg County)

Five

Elizabeth, Chantilly, and Plaza-Midwood:

Moving East

The Elizabeth neighborhood was created as the first suburb to the east of town, following the pattern Dilworth initiated to the south. Elizabeth, which soon expanded to envelope the Rosemont neighborhood, was then joined on the east side by Plaza-Midwood and Chantilly, giving momentum to development eastward that continues today.

Compare this grand, bungalow-style showplace with the other small homes on Clement Avenue in Elizabeth and with those throughout Plaza-Midwood and Chantilly: there are more similarities than differences. Appealing roof, porch, and window details make this styling truly classic. This house was built by John Baxter Alexander, the brother of Elizabeth developer Walter S. Alexander, who built a similar house for himself next door. The house was occupied by its original owner until his death in 1943. In later years, it became a boarding house, and was eventually divided into five condominium residences. (*The Charlotte Observer*)

Elizabeth Avenue was once a street of proud residences that served as the grand entrance to the neighborhood that shared its name. Over the years, the avenue has gradually become a commercial corridor with no remaining private homes. This early 1930s view gives a sense of Elizabeth Avenue in its early days. (Duke Power Archives)

The smartly attired operator of this electrical substation stands ready at the switch that controlled electric power to the Elizabeth neighborhood. Charlotte's early suburbs owed much of their success to the mutually beneficial cooperation between real estate developers and local utilities. The Southern Power Company played a key role in the ability of these new neighborhoods to lure residents out of the town center and into Dilworth, Elizabeth, Myers Park, and their sister suburbs. This photograph was taken around 1910. (Duke Power Archives)

What a luxury it was to have laundry pick-up and delivery! Roland S. Ferguson, shown here around 1920, operated the Sanitary Steam Laundry, which is believed to have been located on North Cecil Street near the Elizabeth neighborhood. The prosperous business boasted two telephone numbers. (Robinson-Spangler Carolina Room, Public Library of Charlotte and Mecklenburg County)

This fine, Neo-Classical-style house was considered to be Charlotte's last remaining center city mansion when it was demolished in the early 1990s. The Elizabeth Avenue home was built in 1903 by H.T. McKinnon for his daughter and son-in-law, and remained a private residence until 1964, when it was converted into the Edmor Motor Inn. Some of the building's elaborate trim work was sold as salvage, and now embellishes other homes and gardens in Charlotte. (*The Charlotte Observer*)

Central High School has played a key role in the educational history of Charlotte. It was built in the 1920s at the intersection of Elizabeth Avenue and Cecil Street (now Kings Drive). Here, in the building that stands at the entrance to the Elizabeth neighborhood, night classes were first offered for GIs returning from World War II. From those beginnings, Charlotte College came to be. Today, the Central High School building is part of the Central Piedmont Community College. Under the determined leadership of educator Dr. Bonnie Cone, the old Charlotte College evolved into the University of North Carolina at Charlotte. (The Charlotte Observer)

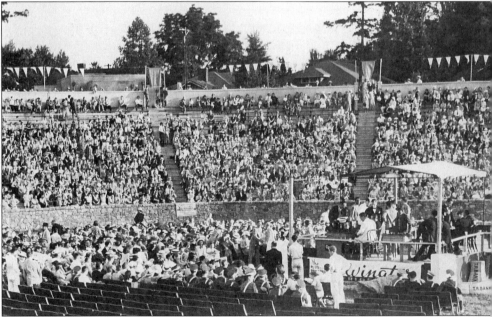

Built on the edge of Elizabeth as part of Independence Park, Memorial Stadium has been the scene of a broad variety of public gatherings since 1936. Best known as the site of the annual Shrine Bowl game between North and South Carolina high school football all-stars, Memorial Stadium has also hosted festivals, political rallies, holiday pageants, and concerts. Here, a large crowd has turned out for an electric appliance promotion in the late 1930s held in one corner of the stadium. (Duke Power Archives)

Homes in the Elizabeth and Chantilly neighborhoods quickly took root in Charlotte's green farmland, and so did the trees planted there. Compare this more modern view of Bay Street to the 1936 view of Shenandoah Avenue with its first house (following page), just a few short blocks away. The varying roof heights and lines add visual interest to the streetscape, making this area as appealing today as is was when it was young. (*The Charlotte Observer*)

They're as popular today as they were sixty years ago. The bungalow-style home could be built in a variety of sizes and styles and with a variety of materials. Whether wood-sided, brick, or stucco, cozy or spacious, the bungalow has endured. Look closely at the four separate porch roofs at the left of this photograph: while appearing to define four separate structures, they all belong to the same building. The creative combinations of porches, columns, trim, and roof details, and the varying distances between the houses and the street, create an inviting vista along this Elizabeth roadway. (*The Charlotte Observer*)

There was only one other house on Shenandoah Avenue when the Pearre family built theirs, remembers Mary Pearre, who has lived in her Chantilly home since 1936. "It was a cornfield," she says. Mary and her husband George were married over in the Dilworth neighborhood, "in the parsonage," she recalls, then moved to their new home, away from town a bit, and just inside the city limits. The streets were red dirt and there were no street lights, but that didn't stop Mary and George Pearre from enjoying their 1936 four-door Dodge automobile, shown here parked in front of the house. Sixty years later, Mary still remembers the color: "Stratosphere Blue!" she laughs. (Mary Pearre)

This early 1950s view of the corner of The Plaza and Commonwealth Avenue shows a section of what was then considered part of the Chantilly neighborhood. The development of Independence Boulevard just a few blocks away changed the character of this and other sections of the city from residential to commercial. (Kugler's Studio)

72

Harry Golden was one of Charlotte's best-known adopted sons. For years, he published his personal journal, the *Carolina Israelite*, from his home and office on Elizabeth Avenue. Golden, a native New Yorker, moved to Charlotte in 1941 and embarked on a writing career that would include twenty books and countless essays, many using his biting wit to fight racial segregation. His close friendship with Carl Sandburg brought the poet to Charlotte often, and Golden became Sandburg's biographer and literary executor. Even though Golden's home and office, pictured here, were lost in a fire, the author moved a few blocks away where he continued to live and write until his death in 1981. (*The Charlotte Observer*)

The Plaza has retained much of its original character, from the stately VanLandingham House to these simple yet elegant Craftsman-style bungalows. Because of its distance from the center of town, interest in the new Plaza neighborhood, originally part of Chatham Estates, was initially less intense than in other streetcar suburbs. Though the neighborhood's popularity has ebbed and flowed through the years, the result has been an area that remains architecturally and economically diverse. (John Reynolds Rogers Jr.)

This wide intersection at The Plaza and Parkwood Road marked the end of the streetcar line that served Plaza-Midwood, Chatham Estates, and the northern end of the Chantilly neighborhood. The trolley ran down the broad median of The Plaza, which had been planted with grass by the early 1950s when this photograph was taken. Today, the median blooms with flowers and trees, distinguishing The Plaza as one of Charlotte's most notable avenues. (Robinson-Spangler Carolina Room, Public Library of Charlotte and Mecklenburg County)

Six
Belmont and
North Charlotte:
Mill Communities

The textile mill communities that developed north of central Charlotte around the turn of the century are in many ways the best preserved of the city's older neighborhoods. The working-class character and often simple, yet sound, homes of North Charlotte and Belmont still look much as they did in their early days.

Even though more than fifty years have passed since the trolley ran through North Charlotte, the Hand Pharmacy building still stands on North Davidson Street. Since its completion around 1912, the two-story brick structure has maintained its presence as a community landmark; it once housed a union hall on its second floor. As the rest of the block slowly filled in with a bank of stores, a solid retail district was created to serve the mill community that made its home on nearby streets. (*The Charlotte Observer*)

In 1936, when the North Charlotte fire station opened, it contained two jail cells in addition to its usual features. No one is certain if there was a specific incident that made the holding cells necessary, but North Charlotte's distance from the main police station downtown was probably a factor in the decision. (*The Charlotte Observer*)

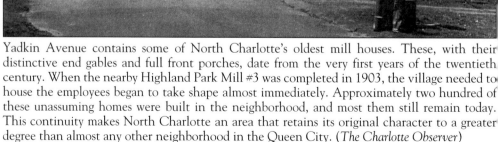

Yadkin Avenue contains some of North Charlotte's oldest mill houses. These, with their distinctive end gables and full front porches, date from the very first years of the twentieth century. When the nearby Highland Park Mill #3 was completed in 1903, the village needed to house the employees began to take shape almost immediately. Approximately two hundred of these unassuming homes were built in the neighborhood, and most them still remain today. This continuity makes North Charlotte an area that retains its original character to a greater degree than almost any other neighborhood in the Queen City. (*The Charlotte Observer*)

Look closely behind toddler Robert Wilson to see Shue's boarding house in North Charlotte. Run by Ceola Shue, it provided housing to many—even some of the ball players who came to town to play on the Highland Park Mill team. Robert's mother, Bessie Christenbury, died just one week after he was born. (Lois Moore Yandle)

The Moore family "always told stories growing up," says Lois Moore Yandle, shown here in the 1930s holding her cousin, Robert Wilson, and kneeling next to her sister Evelyn. "I lived in North Charlotte my whole life until I was married," she says. Today, Mrs. Yandle remembers those stories with a clarity most of us would envy. She began researching her family's past around 1981, but branched out into exploring her neighborhood's history in earnest around 1993, when she read an article that inspired her to seek out photographs from the Moore family's past, some of which appear in this book. (Lois Moore Yandle)

The North Charlotte neighborhood has grown, flourished, declined—and is now enjoying a rebirth as a National Register Historic District. Once the home of a thriving mill community, North Charlotte's streets bore appropriate names, such as "Warp" and "Card." The Highland Inn, with its decorative front windows, is shown here on North Alexander Street. It was built around 1903, the same time the mills were establishing the surrounding village for their workers. (*The Charlotte Observer*)

North Charlotte families, like so many others in Charlotte's growing suburbs, established a strong sense of community and permanence in their neighborhood. Handwritten notes and old newspaper clippings that recorded graduations, weddings, and church reunions overlap with familiar family names: Berryhill, Russell, Lofton, Haithcock, Cook, and Turbyfill (the more common North Charlotte spelling of this name was Turbeville). In this photograph, taken during World War I, members of the Stutts family pose on their front porch. (Lois Moore Yandle)

The North Charlotte Primary School was the backdrop for this 1930s photograph. Although no one has been able to positively identify the dark-suited man and the woman next to him, the man wearing a vested suit is Joe Moore. Standing next to him is his lifelong friend and North Charlotte neighbor, Charlie Stutts. (Lois Moore Yandle)

The fact that so many houses of this style survive is a testament to their practicality and affordability. The streets of North Charlotte were lined with small homes like these that were built to house families employed by the Highland Park Company's mills. Two streets bear the names of area developers Holt and Spencer; one named for a third, Charles W. Johnston, bears his first name rather than his last. The home seen in this photograph still stands today at 924 Charles Street. (John Reynolds Rogers Jr.)

This early panoramic view shows the Men's Bible Class in front of the Spencer Memorial United Methodist Church, located on North Davidson Street, on the site of the present North Charlotte YMCA. It was named for J.S. Spencer, one of the original developers of Highland Park Mill #3 and its surrounding mill village. Although the church was razed in the 1950s, the

The 1911 Spencer Memorial Church, a warm, brick structure with Gothic Revival detailing, was demolished in the 1950s to make way for the Johnston YMCA. This early postcard shows the church, along with one of the congregation's early ministers. (Lois Moore Yandle)

congregation is still active in the neighborhood at a newer sanctuary on East Thirty-Sixth Street. (Robinson-Spangler Carolina Room, Public Library of Charlotte and Mecklenburg County)

Sometimes, the most unassuming images reveal details of the past that could easily be forgotten were it not for these valuable documents. This extremely rare informal portrait is one of the few known photographs that remain of the North Charlotte business district in the late 1920s. Mr. Gamble, proprietor of Gamble's Pharmacy, poses in front of one of his two shops, this one on North Davidson Street near Thirty-Sixth Street. This store was located one block south of another North Charlotte landmark, the Hand Pharmacy. Gamble's Pharmacy later became Horn's Shoe Shop. (Lois Moore Yandle)

Monday was the weekly wash day for many families. Here, Mary Madeline Moore scrubs laundry in an outdoor tub, accompanied by, from left to right, daughter Evelyn Moore, neighbor Buster Suddreth, and niece Peggy Christenbury. Another daughter, Lois Moore Yandle (not pictured) remembers that her father built a storm shed behind their Charles Avenue home near the laundry, to protect the family if they were caught washing clothes when a sudden storm came up. (Lois Moore Yandle)

"I went to work at the mill when I was fourteen years old," remembers Woodrow Austin. "My whole family worked there." This portrait of the spinning and warping departments of Highland Park Mill #3 was made in March of 1928. Sixteen years old at the time, Austin is the dark-haired young man at the far right of the top row. Mill life extended far beyond the workplace—mill owners built the houses in which their workers lived and the churches where they worshiped. But everyone who lived in a mill village remembers the sports teams. Outfielder Woodrow Austin recalls taking part in what was known as "the Black-and-White game," believed to be the first "mixed" game in the South, around 1933.

The mill employees shown here are, from left to right, as follows: (bottom row) Zoe Jarvis, Ida Austin, Clara Hollingsworth, Mrs. Tom Kimball, Mamie Riddles, Dazie Riddles, Evelyn Wise, Jewel Lee Marshan, Jollie Belle Wilson, and Zoe Marshan; (second row) ? Jones, Mrs. John Barrett, Catherine Helms, Tessie Helms, Annie Parker, ? Hord, Mary Davis, Alberta Davis, Tiny Setzer, Lucille Johnson, Jim Osborne, Sue Wise, Holly Farrington, Liza Moore, Annie Helms, Maggie Parker, and Callie Glover; (third row) Mert Price, Lois Fink, Cely ?, Temp Kelly, S. Summers, Annie Williams, Lucy Riddles, Lidy Johnson, Bob McCarter, Dave Parker, Tom Orr, Ralph Austin, Pop Summers, Jim Farrington, ? Davis, Eddie Thomas, and Will Berryhill; (top row) Sid Berryhill, Louis Fink, Bill Parker, Willie Austin, Frank Ballard, Duke Austin, Pop Horton, Floyd Callahan, Earl Helms, ? Brown, Will Penneger, Clyde Summers, John McCorkle, Cal Pope, and Woodrow Austin. (Woodrow Austin)

It resembled no other church in Charlotte when it was built in the Belmont neighborhood. Unlike more predictable styles with their traditional steeples, the original Villa Heights ARP Church boasted a modern, wide-roofed design when it was erected around 1910 on Parkwood Avenue. Today, the commanding brick structure is the home of the Parkwood Institutional CME Church. (John Reynolds Rogers Jr.)

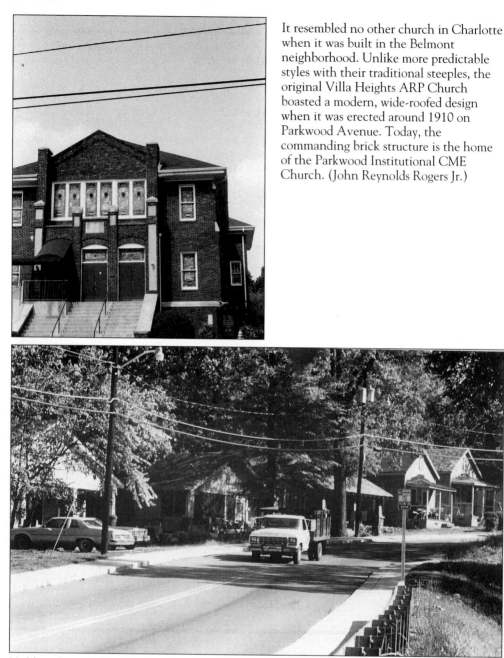

Unlike other neighborhoods where the trolley arrived first and homes followed later, Belmont's turn-of-the-century housing was built to support the neighborhood's three textile mills before trolley lines existed between downtown and Belmont. Since residents could walk to work, it was 1910 before the trolley arrived. But the neighborhood just north of downtown has had to face more than its share of struggles. As the mills began to close or relocate in the 1950s, jobs became scarce. In the 1960s and '70s, urban residential areas such as Brooklyn were reclaimed for commercial development and Belmont became home for a number of the displaced families, leading to a rapid turnover of residents. These Belmont Avenue cottages still survive. (*The Charlotte Observer*)

Seven
The Westside
Neighborhoods:
Biddleville, Washington Heights, Seversville, Wesley Heights, Greenville, and Hoskins

The area that has come to be known as West Charlotte was not always so sharply divided from the city's eastern half. As Trade Street headed west, it connected with old roads such as Beatties Ford Road, which went north toward the Catawba River, and Tuckaseegee Road. These roads became the natural paths of growth to the west.

Biddleville grew up in the 1870s surrounding Biddle Institute, and other neighborhoods evolved, connecting the college to the city. Washington Heights was created as a neighborhood for African Americans; Wesley Heights and Greenville would undergo dramatic demographic shifts in the course of their history. Even the mill village of Hoskins, once remote, would be connected by trolley as Charlotte's west side grew. This 1940s photograph shows how these neighborhoods have struggled with change. At this busy crossroads, automobiles share the road with a horse-drawn cart. (Robinson-Spangler Carolina Room, Public Library of Charlotte and Mecklenburg County)

Johnson C. Smith University began in 1867 in Charlotte's Second Ward as Biddle Institute. Founded by three Northern Presbyterian ministers in the aftermath of the Civil War, the school was established to educate black ministers. Biddle Institute moved to Charlotte's west side in the 1870s, to a site donated by the Myers family. The campus quickly became the centerpiece of a growing African-American community. Biddle Hall, with its distinctive clock tower, was constructed in 1884. In 1923, the school was renamed for Pittsburgh businessman Johnson C. Smith, whose widow contributed in excess of $700,000 to the school in her husband's memory. The Biddle Hall clock tower remains a focal point of the university today. (*The Charlotte Observer*)

These gentlemen, gathered on the steps of Biddle Hall, are the students and graduates of the class of 1892. They attended the theological program at Biddle Institute. Today, the school is known as Johnson C. Smith University. (Robinson-Spangler Carolina Room, Public Library of Charlotte and Mecklenburg County)

Lakewood Park was a favorite with Charlotteans until it closed in the early 1930s. Connected to the center of town by streetcar lines, the park could be reached from almost anywhere in Charlotte. This 1910 view shows the park's trolley station, located on Tuckaseegee Road on the west side. (Duke Power Archives)

Lakewood Park was a popular gathering spot for picnics and band concerts in the 1910s and '20s. Built on the western edge of Charlotte by Edward Dilworth Latta, developer of the Dilworth neighborhood, the park was located near the site where Harding High School stands today. Lakewood boasted a large lake and a small zoo and was accessible from most parts of the city by Latta's trolley system. The Depression hit hard though, and since people had little money to spend on recreation, Lakewood closed in 1933 after a storm destroyed the dam and drained the lake. (*The Charlotte Observer*)

In 1915 Charlotte's African-American community celebrated "The Fiftieth Anniversary of the Freedom of the Negro in the County of Mecklenburg and the City of Charlotte, North Carolina." To commemorate the occasion, civic leader C.H. Watson authored *Colored Charlotte*, a comprehensive resource that described the schools, churches, civic and social organizations, and businesses in the black community. The publication also promoted a new suburb, Washington Heights. This westside neighborhood, which was located on the trolley line, was developed to provide "country" housing for middle-class black families who could afford the trolley fare to and from their jobs in town. Washington Heights is believed to be the only streetcar suburb in the state built specifically for black homeowners. (Second Ward High School National Alumni Foundation)

Nothing else in Charlotte quite compares to the Excelsior Club. Since the 1940s, it has stood on Beatties Ford Road as a social and political gathering place for many westside leaders. From its glass-block windows to its black-striped roof detail to the aluminum awning that shields its entrance, the Excelsior's Art Moderne elements make it truly original. (*The Charlotte Observer*)

lthough Wesley Heights was populated by hite families when the neighborhood was unded, a number of black families found eir way to this westside neighborhood hen they were displaced by urban renewal the 1960s and '70s. In this photograph, e Bethel AME Church of Wesley Heights splays its interesting Romanesque Revival aracteristics. With its triple-arched entry d detailed brick-work, the church was esigned by Louis Asbury, whose work can e seen throughout Charlotte's early burbs. Rather than occupying a site on an ban corridor, the house of worship faces e residential neighborhood from its randin Road corner lot. (John Reynolds ogers Jr.)

Believed to be the first house built in Wesley Heights, this is the Wadsworth House, named for the family on whose farmland the neighborhood was developed. The large home at 400 South Summit Avenue was designed by Louis Asbury and built in 1911. Although Wesley Heights was developed on the borders of Charlotte's urban Third Ward, it was planned as a suburb. Unlike other neighborhoods that have been redeveloped, demolished, or urbanized in recent years, Wesley Heights maintains much of its original appeal. Its pleasant mix of homes large and small, duplexes, four-plexes, and churches form the fabric of a thriving neighborhood. Today, the house that was known as the Wadsworth House is now the Northwest Funeral Home. (John Reynolds Rogers Jr.)

Colonel Macomb and Staff, Camp Greene, N.C., March 14th 1919
— front of Headquarters.

When the United States entered World War I, a U.S. Army training facility was quickly established on Charlotte's west side. Nearly sixty thousand men came through Camp Greene during its brief life, which ended soon after the armistice in November of 1919. Here, Colonel Macomb and his staff pose in March of that same year outside the camp headquarters at the old Dowd farmhouse. The house still stands today on Monument Avenue. (Robinson-Spangler Carolina Room, Public Library of Charlotte and Mecklenburg County)

The Wesley Heights Graded School, located on the neighborhood's South Summit Avenue, was built about 1925 as part of an attempt to draw new families with young children to the area. In penmanship that would certainly have received an "A" from the teacher, the children listed on the back of this undated photograph of the fourth grade include the following: (seated girls) Vergie Evans, Rubie Lee Todd, Martha Auten, Emma Rennie, Margie York, and Elizabeth Teamster; (standing girls) Mabel Wilson, Ethel Godfrey, Delores Holtzclaw, Hazel Lingle, Idelle Davis, Addie House, Mildred Gardner, and Gladys Frazier; (boys) Harold Barber, Kennith Keale, David Edwards, Herman Morgan, Fred Eaton, Roland Asbury, Layton Brown, and Henry Jamison. The school was demolished in the early 1970s. (Robinson-Spangler Carolina Room, Public Library of Charlotte and Mecklenburg County)

Children play on a sandy hillside much like many others found in the Carolinas. Where downtown's West Eleventh Street left the center of Charlotte, it turned due west and followed the railroad line into the Greenville neighborhood. Although the housing styles in Greenville were similar to those found in other parts of town, many homes fell into disrepair and were eventually torn down. Fortunately, the community has been rebuilt and today it maintains an active neighborhood association. (*The Charlotte Observer*)

Greenville and its residents are notable for having been active in Charlotte's early neighborhood preservation efforts. The Queen City has a strong network of community organizations, and as this 1960s photograph shows, Greenville residents were at the forefront of this movement. (*The Charlotte Observer*)

The Seaboard Railroad tracks run along the bottom of this view of Greenville. The neighborhood school is visible at the left of the image. Most of the houses that lined Burton and Oliver Streets in this photograph from around 1960 are gone today, but some sections of Greenville still retain their classic neighborhood scale. (*The Charlotte Observer*)

A 1928 trolley map spelled it "Rozzell's Ferry Road," but on a later map it appears as "Rozzelles Ferry." Either way, the trolley line that followed it north and west out of downtown Charlotte terminated in the Hoskins community, another of the city's important mill villages. The mill itself was built in 1903. Its construction marked the beginning of a career for a young contractor named J.A. Jones, who would later go on to head one of the country's largest construction companies. Although the Hoskins Mill remained shuttered for years, it was recently renovated into rental apartment housing. (*The Charlotte Observer*)

This 1950s aerial view shows Wilkinson Boulevard, looking east toward the center city. The artery has long been one of Charlotte's major access routes to the west side. Even then, this area contained a diverse mixture of residential and industrial buildings. The Southern Engineering steel plant, visible in the foreground, was known locally as "Little Pittsburgh." It still operates on the same site today. Years before the construction of Interstate 85, Wilkinson Boulevard connected Charlotte with its neighbor to the west, Gastonia. (Kugler's Studio)

Eight
Faces and Places

Throughout Charlotte's history the people who have lived and worked here—from mill workers and bankers to teachers and families—have given the city its unique character. Even when growth and the influence of new citizens have altered Charlotte's physical appearance, the city has always retained its central characteristic as a Southern town that values its social traditions.

This group portrait of Charlotte's police officers, taken around 1910, shows a group of civil servants that appear as if they would fit as easily into a neighborhood in the industrial Northeast as in a Carolina Piedmont town. Yet the underlying personality of Charlotte has remained constant. Even as the city attracted famous visitors and acquired the trappings of a major metropolis, Charlotte's people have been its timeless asset. (Robinson-Spangler Carolina Room, Public Library of Charlotte and Mecklenburg County)

GOLD MINING MACHINERY.

MECKLENBURG IRON WORKS,

JOHN WILKES, Manager,

CHARLOTTE, N. C.

Engines, Boilers, Saw Mills.

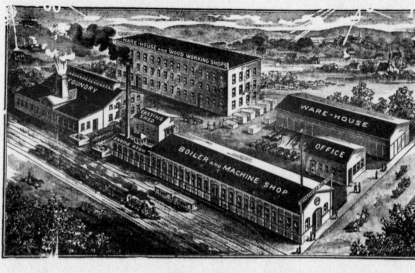

Manufacturers in IRON, STEEL, BRASS and WOOD.

The Mecklenburg Iron Works was one of Charlotte's largest employers in the mid-nineteenth century. Founded by New York native and U.S. Naval Academy graduate John Wilkes, the factory produced iron rails for the Piedmont's thriving railroads, and then used those rail lines to ship its other products to customers throughout the South. During the Civil War, the factory produced cannonballs for the Confederate Army and ship iron for the CSA Navy. When Mrs. Jefferson Davis, the first lady of the Confederacy, fled with her children from Richmond to Charlotte in April of 1865, a number of prominent Charlotte women cared for the family when they arrived. John Wilkes' wife was one of them. (North Carolina Collection, University of North Carolina Library at Chapel Hill)

As Charlotteans celebrated Mecklenburg Declaration Day in May of 1916, they were joined by President Woodrow Wilson and the governors of both Carolinas. Wilson no doubt enjoyed the festivities as a diversion from the ongoing tensions between the United States and Mexico, and from the growing certainty of war in Europe. Less than a year after his visit to Charlotte, Wilson would ask Congress to declare war on Germany, bringing the U.S. into World War I. (*The Charlotte Observer*)

Like the fire departments of many cities, Charlotte kept one of its steam engines long after the era of modern firetrucks had arrived. Here, the horse-drawn Engine #2 takes part in a local parade. (Robinson-Spangler Carolina Room, Public Library of Charlotte and Mecklenburg County)

"Equipped with 12 electric ranges!" someone carefully penned across this 1926 image of Charlotte's Gallagher Apartments, and what a modern convenience they were seventy years ago, when a loaf of bread cost 9¢ and a gallon of gas was 12¢. Although the dwellings pictured here appear as stylish, modern, and comfortable as any being built today, older residents who recall the early days of Charlotte's first "modern" apartments remember, too, the now-outdated coal-burning fireplaces and laundry washtubs that were commonplace. (Duke Power Archives)

The letters on their basketball jerseys stood for Hudson Silk Hosiery, and when their women's basketball team took the city league trophy in 1936, it was no surprise. The mill, which had originally been located on the site of the First Ward School, boasted employees who were energetic and dedicated, both at work and at play. Player #8 was Mary Pearre, who still smiles when she remembers those earlier days. (Mary Pearre)

Even as far back as the 1920s, businesses used a number of novel approaches to advertise their products. In this early 1930s promotion from the Southern Public Utilities Company, a live elephant emphasized the "big" difference a new refrigerator would make in the lives of modern families. (Duke Power Archives)

As in other towns and cities throughout the nation, the women of Charlotte moved into the work force in unprecedented numbers during World War II. This group of women, photographed in 1941, were part of Duke Power Company's corps of meter readers who stepped into their jobs to fill positions left vacant by men serving in the armed forces. After the war ended, as women realized they had the ability to take jobs beyond the traditionally "female" occupations of teaching, nursing, and homemaking, the face of the workplace was forever changed. (Duke Power Archives)

The Hudson Hosiery Mill baseball team pose at one of the entrances to the mill. The team's Louisville Slugger baseball bats are part of the story, too—the men from Hudson Hosiery favored the Joe Cronin and Jimmie Fox models shown here. Mill-sponsored sports teams were popular, and helped give a community identity to the villages. (Mary Pearre)

Long before the NBA and the NFL came to Charlotte, sports played an important part in the city's recreational landscape. There were several city leagues in different sports, including baseball, basketball, and bowling. A number of businesses sponsored teams made up of company employees. Here are two of the Duke Power Company's entries in local basketball competition: the 1925 women's team and the 1940 men's team. (Duke Power Archives)

For many years, Charlotte served as a major distribution center for several large movie studios. Some of the studios, including MGM and Lowe's, had offices in a section of South Church Street known as "Film Row." The presence of these offices helped the city establish itself as a frequent stop for publicity tours. On one such tour in the 1950s, actress Joanne Woodward visited Charlotte. She's shown here having the finishing touches applied to her coiffure by one of Belk's dapper stylists in the store's downtown salon. In 1950, Ronald Reagan made a personal appearance on behalf of General Electric. No one imagined that the film star who held court with a group of local ladies at the Hotel Charlotte would one day become president. (Kugler's Studio)

Minor league baseball has enjoyed a long history in Charlotte, much of it taking place at Crockett Park on the southern edge of the Dilworth neighborhood. Many of the game's greats, including Cal Ripken, Henry Aaron, and Casey Stengel (pictured here in his Yankees cap), made minor league and exhibition stops at the stadium. The wooden Crockett ballpark was destroyed in a spectacular fire in 1985. (Kugler's Studio)

Photographer Rudy Kugler, along with his wife Inez, captured thousands of images of commerce, industry, and daily life in and around Charlotte from the 1940s through the 1980s. Born in Hungary, Rudy Kugler was an immigrant who found himself looking for work when World War II and its demand for raw materials eliminated his job as a rubber salesman in the South. He and his wife, a Georgia native, put down roots in Charlotte as their new photography business caught on. (Kugler's Studio)

Although it relocated several times, Rudy and Inez Kugler's Photolab studio was always part of downtown Charlotte. And as the business district flourished after the war, so did the demand for corporate portraits, aerial photographs, and the documentation of meetings and events. Rudy and Inez Kugler provided all of these. After Rudy's death in 1978, Inez continued to manage the studio until selling it in 1990. Kugler's Studio, still located in what is now called "uptown" Charlotte, is operated today by its new owner, photographer Ken Beebe. (Kugler's Studio)

Mayor Ben Douglas lobbied tenaciously for its construction, and in 1936, Charlotte's Douglas Airport opened. These photographs show the airport as it appeared in the era following World War II. A new terminal was completed in 1982 and has undergone several expansions since. Today, Charlotte Douglas International Airport ranks among the nation's busiest. Although it was begun as a WPA project, the Queen City's airport has forged one of the most powerful links between its past and its future. (Kugler's Studio)

"First Debs of Charlotte—December, 1951" reads the inscription on the back of this photograph. Even though black and white citizens lived side by side and shared their city, for much of Charlotte's history their churches, schools, and businesses were separate. Here, a dozen young women being presented to society make their debut at the height of the winter social season. (Second Ward High School National Alumni Foundation)

"We are taking no sides," the sign in this Park Road grocery store proclaimed. The store owner took advantage of Charlotte's interest in politics in the autumn of 1952 with a weekly contest. Prospective shoppers, who were also prospective voters, were invited to cast a straw vote choosing their favorite candidate. Each week, a name was drawn and the lucky winner was awarded a 60-pound bale of sugar. As these unofficial early election returns during the week of October 4 indicate, the political sentiments of Charlotteans were in line with the rest of the nation. (Kugler's Studio)

"Good leadership—the key to good business" proclaims the sign above the Charlotte Chamber of Commerce's 1955 banquet. Photographs of important civic structures, such as the then-new Charlotte Coliseum, were incorporated into the hall's decor for the event. Close examination reveals at least eight women in the crowd of several hundred men; those numbers would increase dramatically in the following decades as women continued to claim their places in the business community. (Kugler's Studio)

There's not a snowflake in sight even though it's Christmas time at this holiday tree lot sponsored by the Charlotte Eastern Lions Club. The chapter, which raised funds for civic programs, situated its lot on busy Fourth Street to take advantage of commuters traveling from their downtown offices toward the Elizabeth, Myers Park, and Eastover neighborhoods. The banner facing the street traffic offered Christmas trees for $1.50 and up. (Kugler's Studio)

There is nothing extraordinary about this photograph of a clown greeting a crowd of young children at a Charlotte parade, except for the story that lies behind these expressive faces. Photographer Rudy Kugler captured this scene of an unintentionally yet successfully integrated group on film sometime before 1960. And what better place for it: the Carolinas Carousel Parade, which has enjoyed a long tradition of heralding a holiday season in which all Charlotteans are invited to participate. (Kugler's Studio)

Here's Miss America, Ann Drew, waving to the crowd gathered along the parade route. Whether from the brightness of the afternoon sunshine or the brilliance of the beauty queen and her jewels, many of the onlookers are shielding their eyes as Miss America passes by in this 1950s photograph. (Kugler's Studio)

This August 1960 aerial view shows the Charlotte YMCA building near the Dilworth neighborhood. The facility was considered one of the finest in the Southeast. Also visible, at the bottom of the photograph, is much of the surrounding residential area that existed near the YMCA at that time. (Kugler's Studio)

The YMCA building served as the site of many civic functions, such as the 1955 visit to Charlotte by famed journalist Edward R. Murrow, shown here relaxing with his trademark cigarette. (Kugler's Studio)

During the 1960 presidential campaign, Richard Nixon spoke to a large rally at the Charlotte Coliseum, accompanied by his wife Pat. At a reception after the rally, the Nixons mingled with Charlotteans young and old and greeted this girl scout, who would have to wait until 1968 to claim she'd met the president of the United States. (Kugler's Studio)

When it was first completed, the Charlotte Coliseum (now Independence Arena) boasted the world's largest unsupported concrete dome. The coliseum, located on the newly widened Independence Boulevard with the adjacent Ovens Auditorium, quickly became the focal point for sports and entertainment in the Queen City. This aerial photograph, taken as the coliseum and auditorium were nearing completion, reveals an as-yet-undeveloped corridor, along with several new "automobile" suburbs of the day. (Kugler's Studio)

More than eighty children and not one is crying! Santa Claus presides over the Elks Club's annual Christmas party for the children of Chapter 392's members. In this photograph from the late 1950s, even the Christmas tree at the far right of the photograph reflects the style of the times—it's made of the stark, modern, metallic branches that were just becoming popular. (Kugler's Studio)

By the 1950s, many of Charlotte's trees had grown up and matured along with the city's young neighborhoods. At the intersection of present-day Park Road and Kenilworth Road, this small pond was visited by hopeful angler Skip Kugler and a canine friend. The pond has since been filled in and developed as part of an apartment complex. (Carey Kugler)

Nine

Uptown:
Modern Changes and Challenges

Taken looking east across uptown Charlotte in the 1960s, this photograph captures a sense of both the city's past and its future. The trolley cars and dirt streets of earlier days have gradually been replaced by two generations of skyscrapers and an expanding business center. An even newer version of the center city is on the horizon, however, as many of the buildings shown here will be replaced by the towers of a still-evolving skyline.

With the economic boom of the post-war era, the city emerged as a banking and service industry center, and the appearance of uptown Charlotte changed forever. (Kugler's Studio)

Charlotte's motorcycle police force poses proudly in front of the 1925 city hall. Designed by Charles Christian Hook, the structure is the oldest surviving civic building in what is now the Charlotte-Mecklenburg Government Center area. City hall, and the adjacent 1928 Mecklenburg County Courthouse, were situated on the Second Ward side of East Trade Street, just outside the neighborhood known as Brooklyn. (Kugler's Studio)

Holiday lights illuminate South Tryon Street in this 1950s view. The decorations add to the evening glitter already provided by the many brightly lit signs that drew Charlotteans downtown at night. The neon flame burns steadily outside Piedmont Natural Gas, while two Indian-head columns invite shoppers to browse at Frank Woods Pontiac. Many of the stores recognizable in this image have long since moved to other locations. Others, such as the Fidelity Soda Grill (just behind the car dealership), are only memories today. (Kugler's Studio)

116

One of the complaints often heard from modern-day Charlotteans is that there is no nightlife after the work day ends. This 1940 panoramic photograph shows the throngs of shoppers that have turned out to see the holiday lights turned on. With the Professional Building visible in the foreground, Tryon Street is illuminated by decorated arches that create a canopy of light. (Duke Power Archives)

Charlotte has been the site of a branch of Richmond's Federal Reserve Bank since 1927, and this was a significant factor in the city's development as one of the nation's largest banking centers. As a major corporate employer, the Federal Reserve Bank drew together people of differing backgrounds. These two photographs illustrate a common occurrence in the South of the 1950s—segregated Christmas parties. Above, black partygoers gather around a piano at their celebration; below, an accordion player serenades a table of white partygoers. (Kugler's Studio)

This 1950s view, taken looking north on Tryon Street, shows the sloped walls of Charlotte's Egyptian-Revival Masonic Temple in the foreground. The temple, built in 1913 from a design by two of Charlotte's most noted architects, C.C. Hook and W.G. Rogers, was one of the city's most distinctive structures until its demolition in the 1980s. On the opposite side of the street, a variety of structures defined Charlotte's business center in that day. The Johnston Building, the tall building nearest the foreground on the left, remains today as a key element in Charlotte's ever-changing skyline. (Kugler's Studio)

This section of South Tryon Street has changed dramatically since this early 1950s view was captured. Virtually every structure on the west side of this south-facing picture is gone today. However, the area still plays a vital role in the dynamic of downtown Charlotte. It serves as the location for the city's daily newspaper, *The Charlotte Observer* and remains an essential corridor between two of the city's newest civic facilities: the Charlotte Convention Center and Ericsson Stadium. The photograph also illustrates that Charlotte's reputation for traffic congestion is not a recent phenomenon. (Kugler's Studio)

The Mayfair Hotel, now the Dunhill Hotel, was designed by noted Charlotte architect Louis Asbury, and completed in 1929. This 1950s photograph, although printed from a damaged negative, shows the important street presence of the Mayfair as it anchors the intersection of North Tryon and Sixth Streets. (Kugler's Studio)

With its large, marbled lobby and mirrored ballroom, the Hotel Charlotte reigned for decades as the city's most prestigious lodging. It was constructed in the 1930s and stood at the corner of West Trade and South Poplar Streets, where it played host to visiting actors, musicians, sports celebrities, and presidents. Age and competition took their toll on the hotel, and it was demolished in the 1980s to make way for the Carillon Building. (Kugler's Studio)

The movie marquee advertises Mickey Rooney and Lewis Stone starring in *Judge Hardy's Children*. This 1938 Christmas-time photograph shows the variety of shops and activities found in Charlotte's bustling downtown business district. Look closely to see Garibaldi and Bruns jewelers and the National Hat Shop (right), the Astor Cafe (left), and a banner promoting an upcoming football game overhead. (Duke Power Archives)

As the predominant local retailer in Charlotte, Belk Brothers department store was always working to hold that position through contests and other promotional techniques. In this early 1950s photograph, a lucky Belk's patron is awarded the keys to a new Ford automobile—right in the middle of the store's silver and fine china department! (Kugler's Studio)

The Carolinas Motor Club (the American Automobile Association's affiliate in Charlotte) has had a long and visible presence here. In the days when drivers were required to renew their license tags on the first of each year, the AAA office would help distribute the tags. These photographs show license tag renewal day on January 3, 1950. The long lines (shown above), combined with January's chilly temperatures, created a crush of customers inside the club's South Tryon Street office (shown below). The annual event was later replaced by today's system of staggered renewals throughout the year. (Kugler's Studio)

This "modern" South Tryon Street building served as the home of North Carolina National Bank in the 1960s and early 1970s. The bank's lineage dates back to 1874 and the founding of the Commercial National Bank, the first federally chartered bank in North Carolina. A series of mergers eventually led to the creation in 1960 of North Carolina National Bank. As that institution later expanded beyond the state, its name was changed to NCNB. In 1991, NCNB merged with C&S/Sovran, and NationsBank came into being as one the three largest banks in the U.S. (*The Charlotte Observer*)

Just down South Tryon Street from its competition was Union National Bank. It was one of Charlotte's financial institutions that survived the Depression, largely due to the calm and determined leadership of its then-president, H.M. Victor. After a merger in 1959, Union National, shown here in 1959, became First Union. Today, along with NationsBank, Wachovia, and a host of smaller institutions, First Union has helped Charlotte achieve its status as the premier financial center of the Southeast. (*The Charlotte Observer*)

This Neo-Classical-style building was home to *The Charlotte Observer* and *The Charlotte News* until the Knight Publishing Company relocated to its current modern facility. Although *The Charlotte Observer*'s history dates back well into the nineteenth century, the newspaper's name came about in 1892 when then-owner D.A. Tompkins re-christened the *Charlotte Chronicle* the *Charlotte Daily Observer*. The city's evening newspaper, *The Charlotte News*, was founded in 1888, and boasted such well-known writers as Charles Kuralt and W.J. Cash, who authored his landmark book, *The Mind of the South*, while living in Charlotte. The two papers were separate enterprises until 1959, when Knight Publishing, owner of *The Charlotte Observer*, purchased *The Charlotte News*. Although the evening paper ceased publication in the early 1980s, *The Charlotte Observer*, now part of Knight-Ridder, remains the largest daily-circulation newspaper in the Carolinas. (*The Charlotte Observer*)

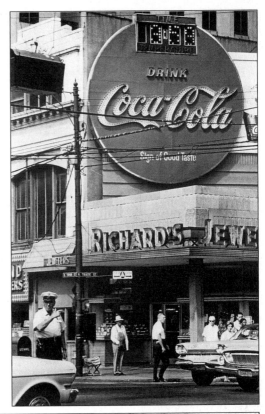

These two snapshots captured in an informal manner the typical pedestrian traffic around 1960 at the Square. As these images illustrate, the importance of the intersection of Trade and Tryon Streets made it a true crossroads for Charlotteans from all quarters of the city. This critical role would be lost in the following decades as Charlotte's retail hub moved to the suburbs and the new shopping malls developing there. (Photograph above, *The Charlotte Observer*; below, Robinson-Spangler Carolina Room, Public Library of Charlotte and Mecklenburg County)

Acknowledgments

Although it would be impossible to tell the entire story of Charlotte in this book, we are most grateful to those who so kindly shared with us photographs, resource materials, and memories. They allowed us to bring to life their personal and collective experiences.

The staff at the Robinson-Spangler Carolina Room at the Public Library of Charlotte and Mecklenburg County helped us locate and identify rare photographs. We are grateful to Margo Fesperman and Shelia Bumgarner, and the Virtual Library's Colleen Beale, whose expert grasp of technology made possible the use of archival photographs. Special thanks must go to Kathryn Frye, whose knowledge of Charlotte's history and how to tell it was inspirational.

We thank publisher Rolfe Neill of *The Charlotte Observer* for allowing us access to the most important photographic documentation of our city's modern history. Mary Newsom, Carlton Montgomery, and Dannye Romine Powell were most helpful, and we thank Ann Bryant, who guided us through the resources in *The Observer*'s library.

The Second Ward High School National Alumni Foundation, its members and supporters, were crucial to the thoroughness of our efforts.

At Duke Power Company, we thank Joe Maher of Corporate Communications, Cathy Stiles, and especially Dennis Lawson, Manager of Document Management Services, for making available to us their organization's exceptional resources.

We thank Ken Beebe of Kugler's Studio, who so patiently allowed us to share his workplace for many hours as we researched and processed numerous photographs.

Photographic Archivists Jerry Cotten and Fred Stipe and Reference Historian Deborah Perotti, all of the Wilson Library at the University of North Carolina at Chapel Hill, answered our every request quickly and accurately. Rosemary Arneson, Director of the Everett Library at Queens College, directed us to publications that could be found nowhere else. At Johnson C. Smith University, Reginald Douglas and Audrey Miller of the James B. Duke Library assisted us.

Many people shared their time, effort, and advice, and for their help we are grateful to: Reggie Adams, Mildred Alridge, Wanda Birmingham, Nora Black, Dorothy Flagg, Heidi Flick and Will MacDonald, Frye Gaillard, Janet Karner, Mildred Mosley, Charles Redfearn, Dick Ridley, Glenda Woolf, and Mike Yonkovig. John Barringer and the staff at Little Professor Book Center, our friends as well as our colleagues, supported this project as they have our others—with understanding and good humor.

Our most heartfelt thanks go to those individuals who lent us their personal photographs: Woodrow Austin, Mary Pearre, and Sandra Pearre; and especially Lois Moore Yandle, whose memories and photographs of North Charlotte document so compellingly that community's unique history.

Finally, two individuals must be recognized, not only for their contributions to this project, but for their commitment to Charlotte's history, their tireless and generous energy, and their willingness to teach others about the importance of community. Vermelle Ely, Archive Chairperson of the Second Ward High School Alumni Foundation, remembers Charlotte's past with astonishing clarity. Her perspective added depth and dignity to this work, and we thank her for her genuine vision. Carey Kugler, the son of photographers Rudy and Inez Kugler, not only made available to us every photograph we needed, but spent hours sorting, identifying, and reproducing these images with us. Without his help, this book would not have been possible.

783C11 FM 953
02/08/00 166010 SELB